I0489012

Visit my website at http://www.coffeeandcoloring.com

View my Etsy shop at http://www.artbyericah.etsy.com

Like my page on Facebook
http://www.facebook.com/coffeeandcoloring

Hi there. My name is Erica Henry and I am the illustrator of *Inspired by Nature*. I'm so glad that you decided to purchase a copy of my book. I have spent hours hand drawing each of these designs for you, and now it is your turn to grab your art supplies and turn them into your own creations.

I have included some blank pages in this book so you can take them out and use them as a protection page as a precautionary measure to prevent bleed through when using markers or gel pens.

Please visit my website at http://www.coffeeandcoloring.com and say hi. I also have tutorials there as well. I love to see your coloring pages that you've done so please post them to Facebook page http://www.facebook.com/coffeeandcoloring.

I want to give a big shout out to the wonderful members of the Facebook group, Coloring for Stress Relief and Enjoyment. They have been so supportive of me along the entire creation of *Inspired by Nature*. I also want to give

shoutouts to Heidi Berthiaume, Melanie Topp Steeves, Chidchanok Siri, Kiya Boardman, and Lynette Davis-Farnum who have won different coloring challenges featuring my coloring pages.

I hope you are as excited to start this coloring journey, as I was to create the book. Now, grab your coloring supplies and get to coloring

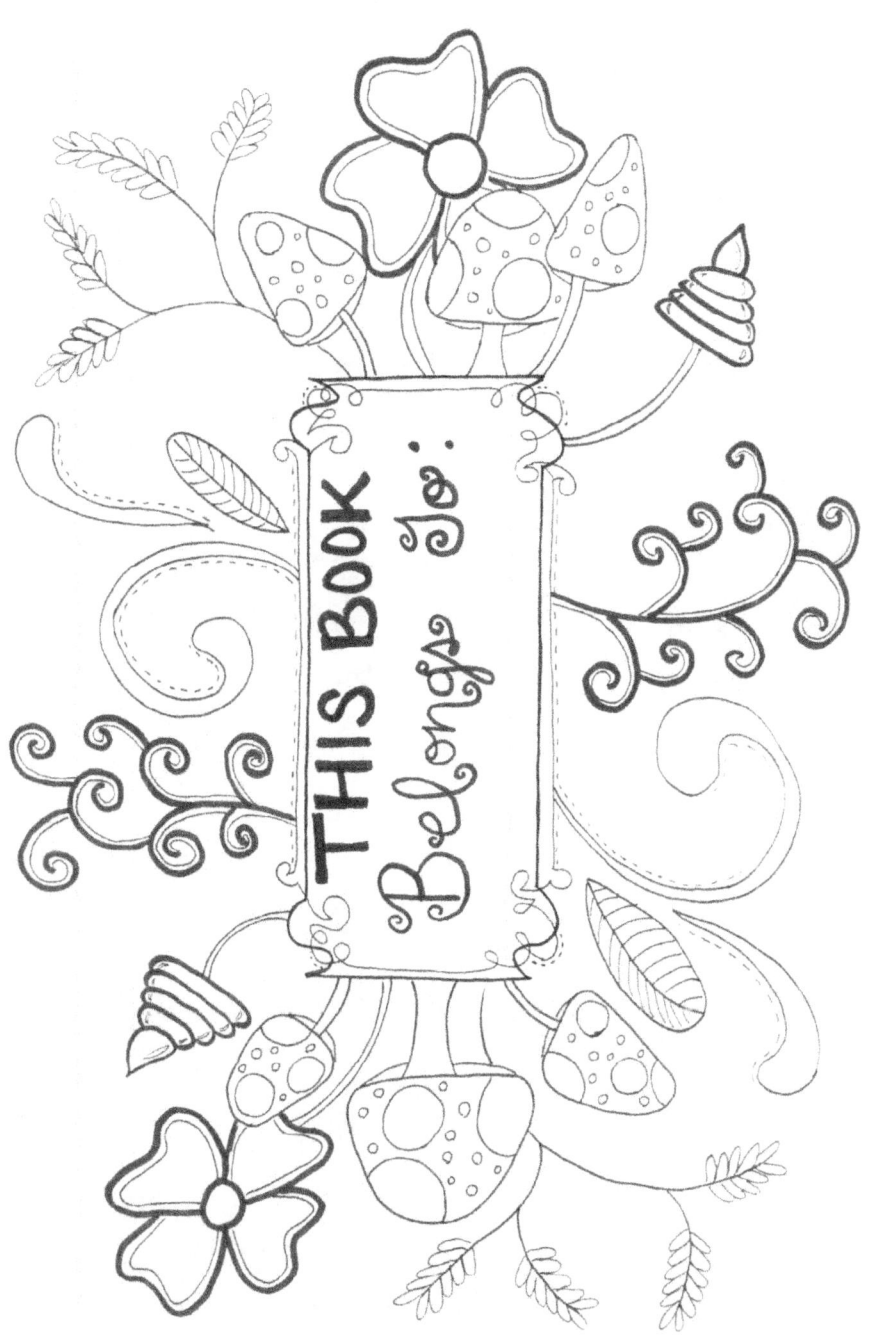

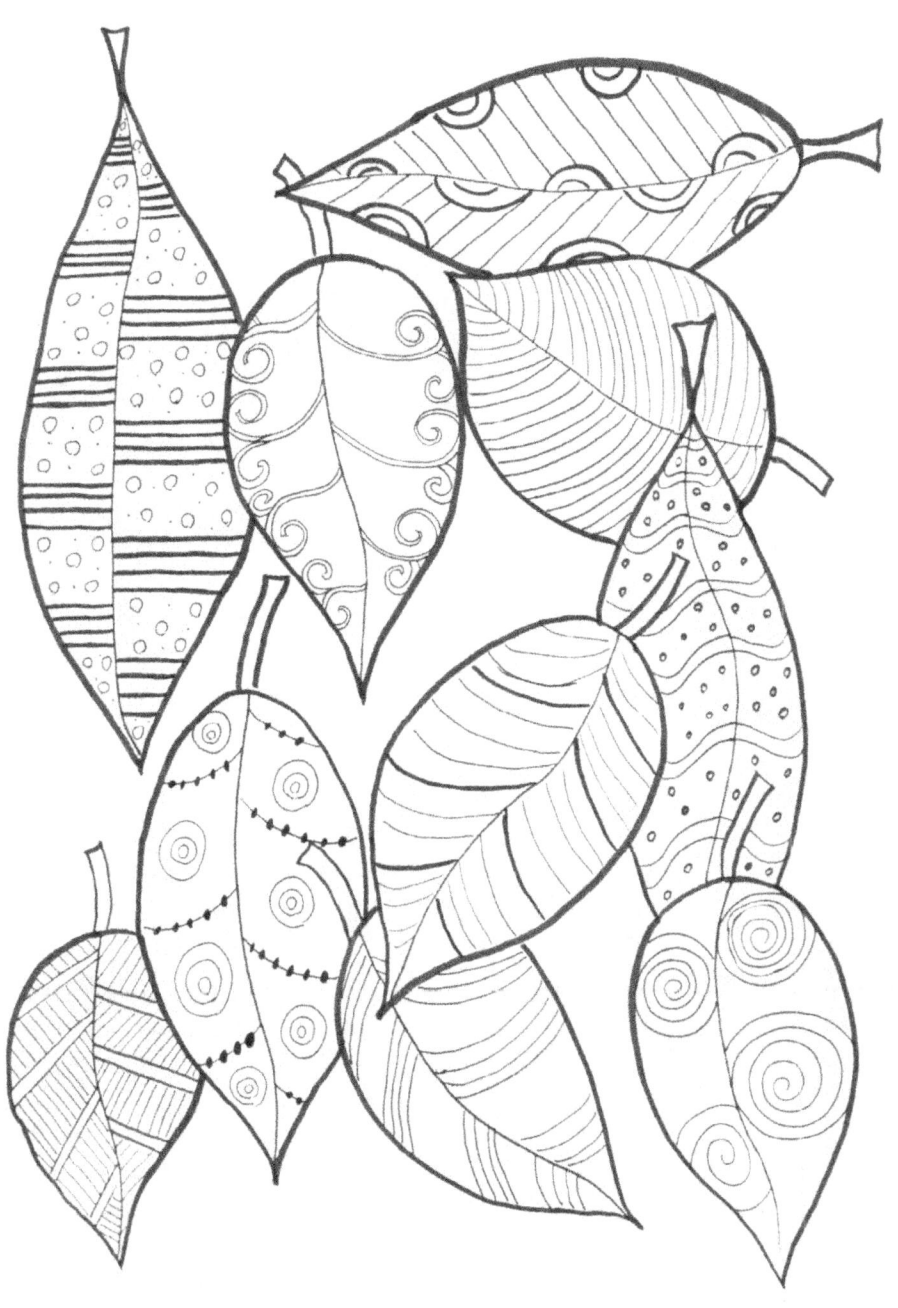

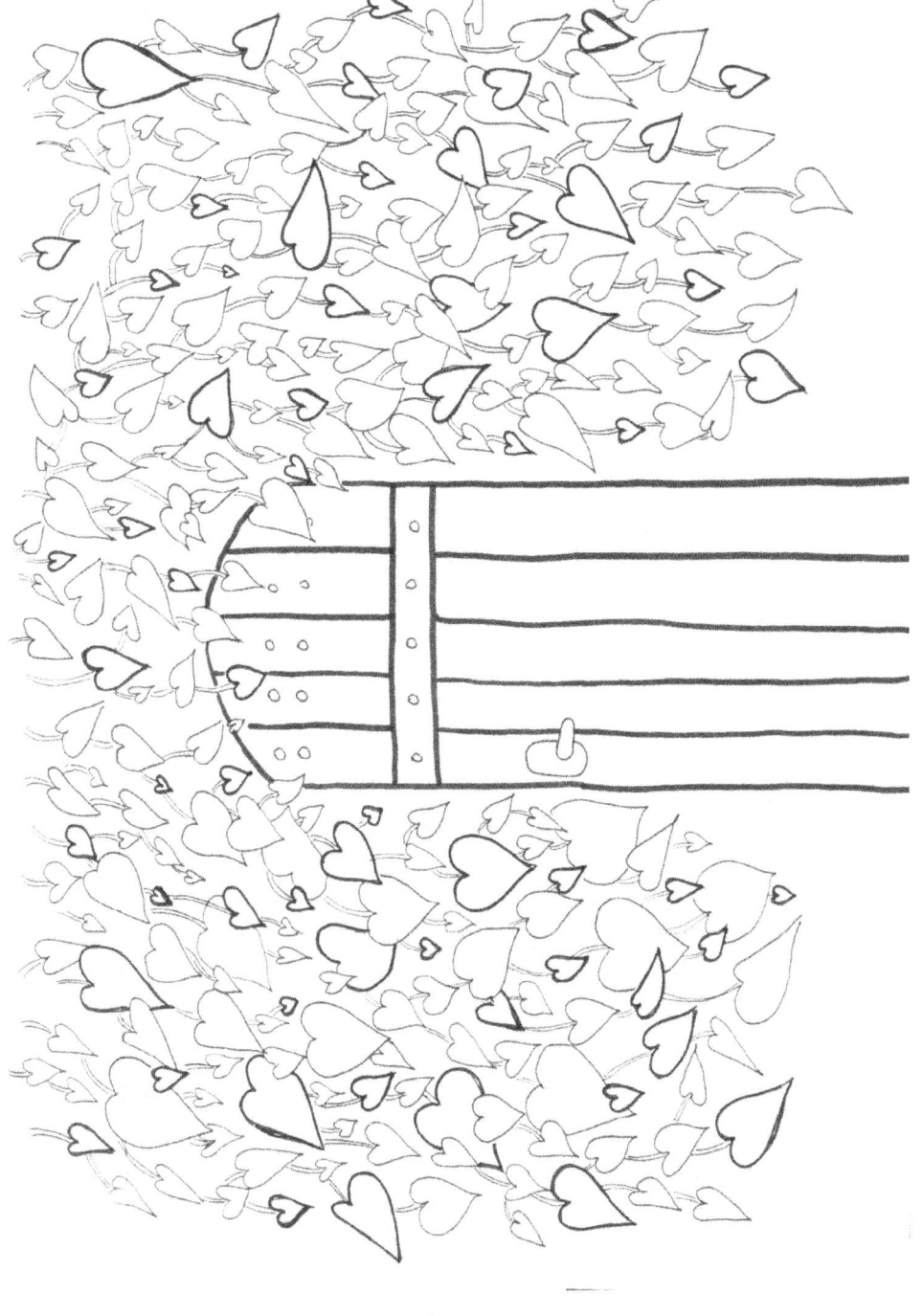

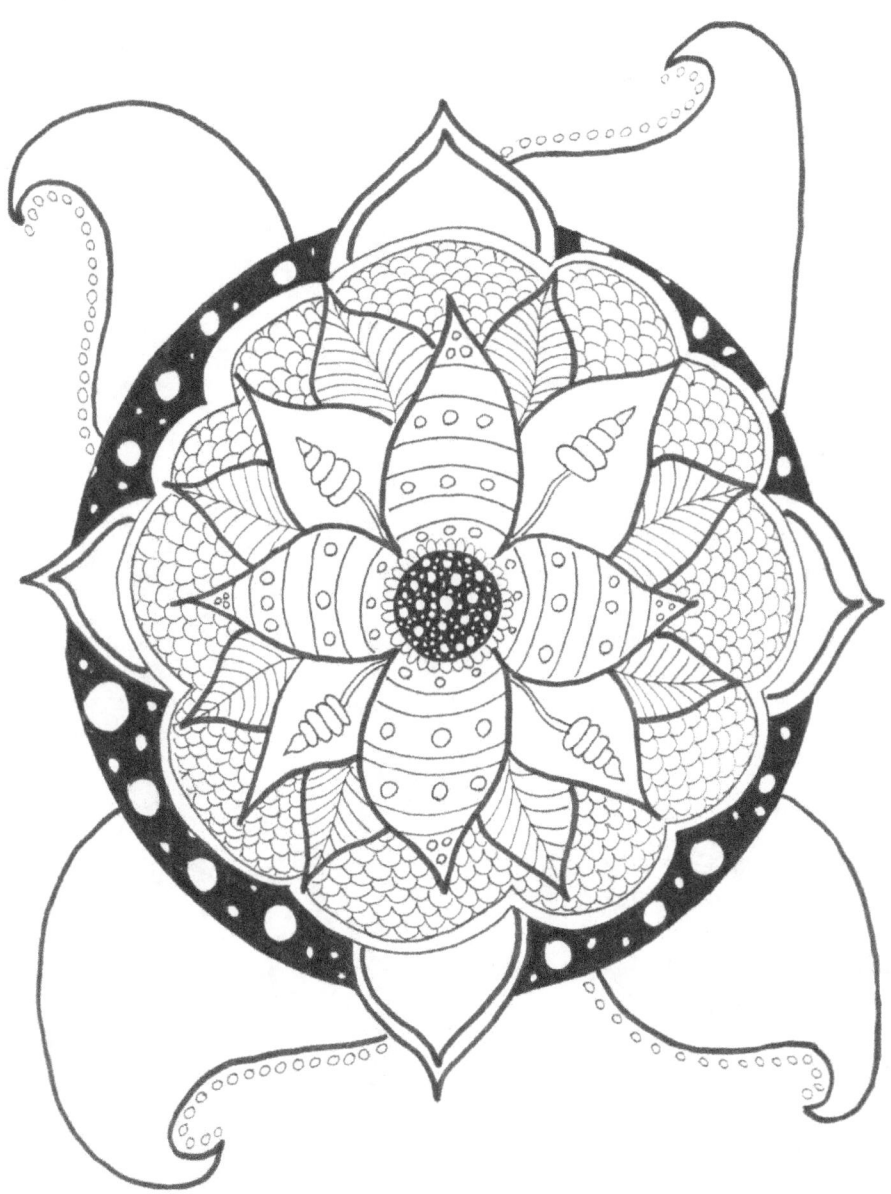

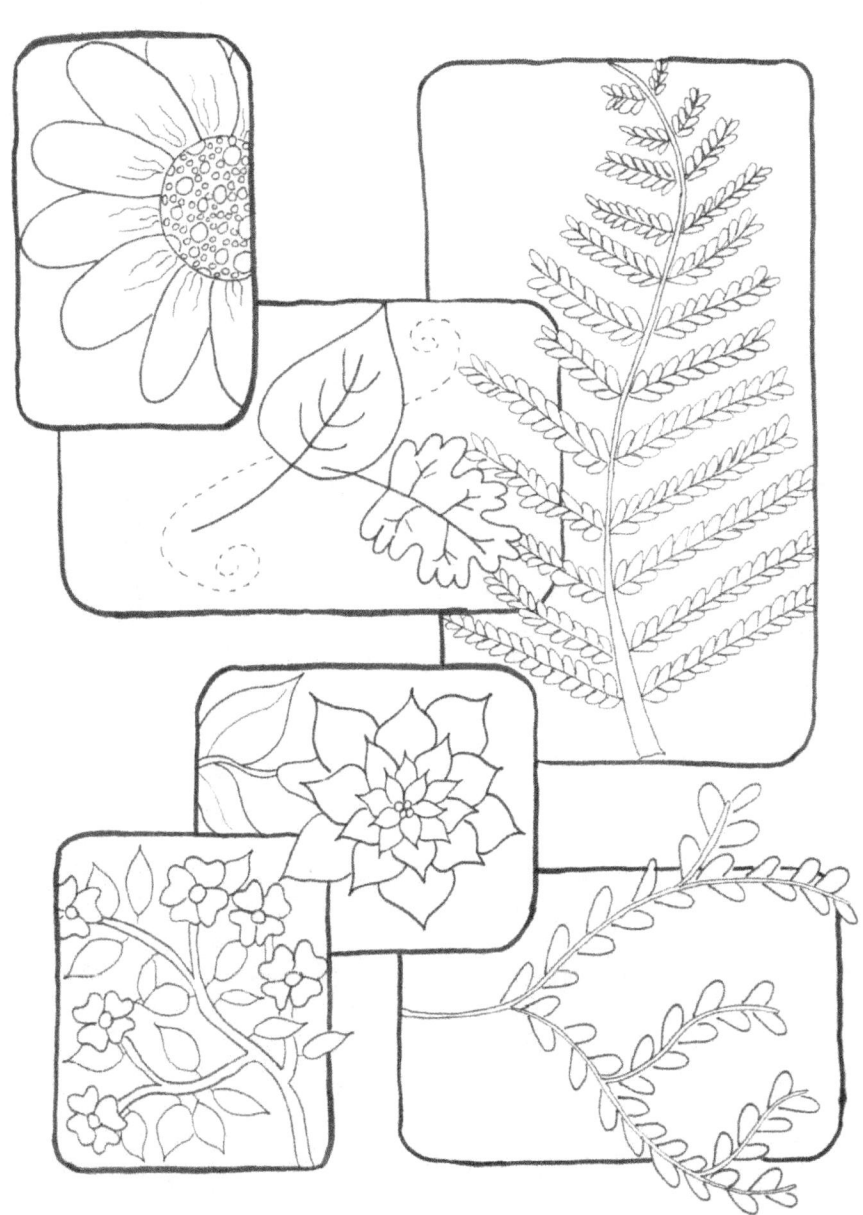

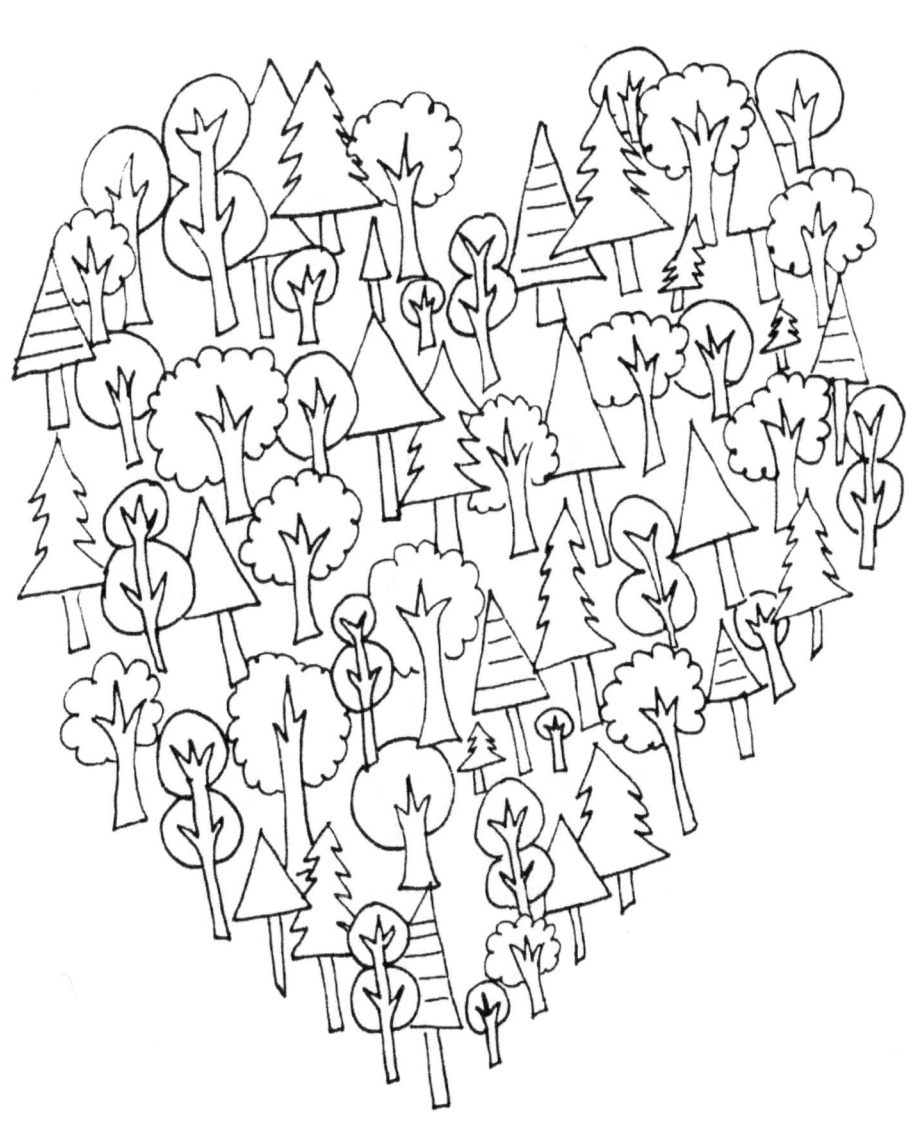

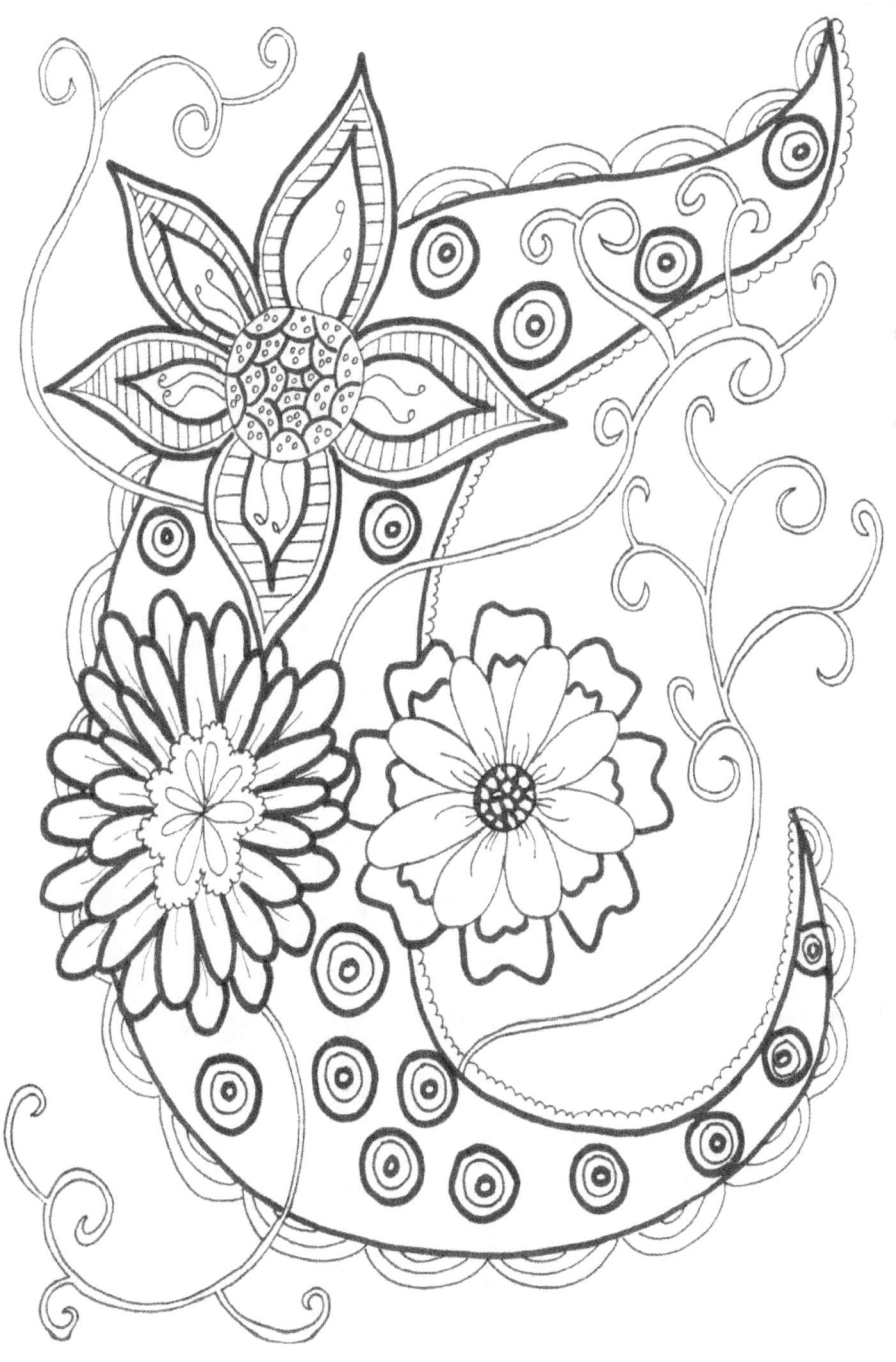

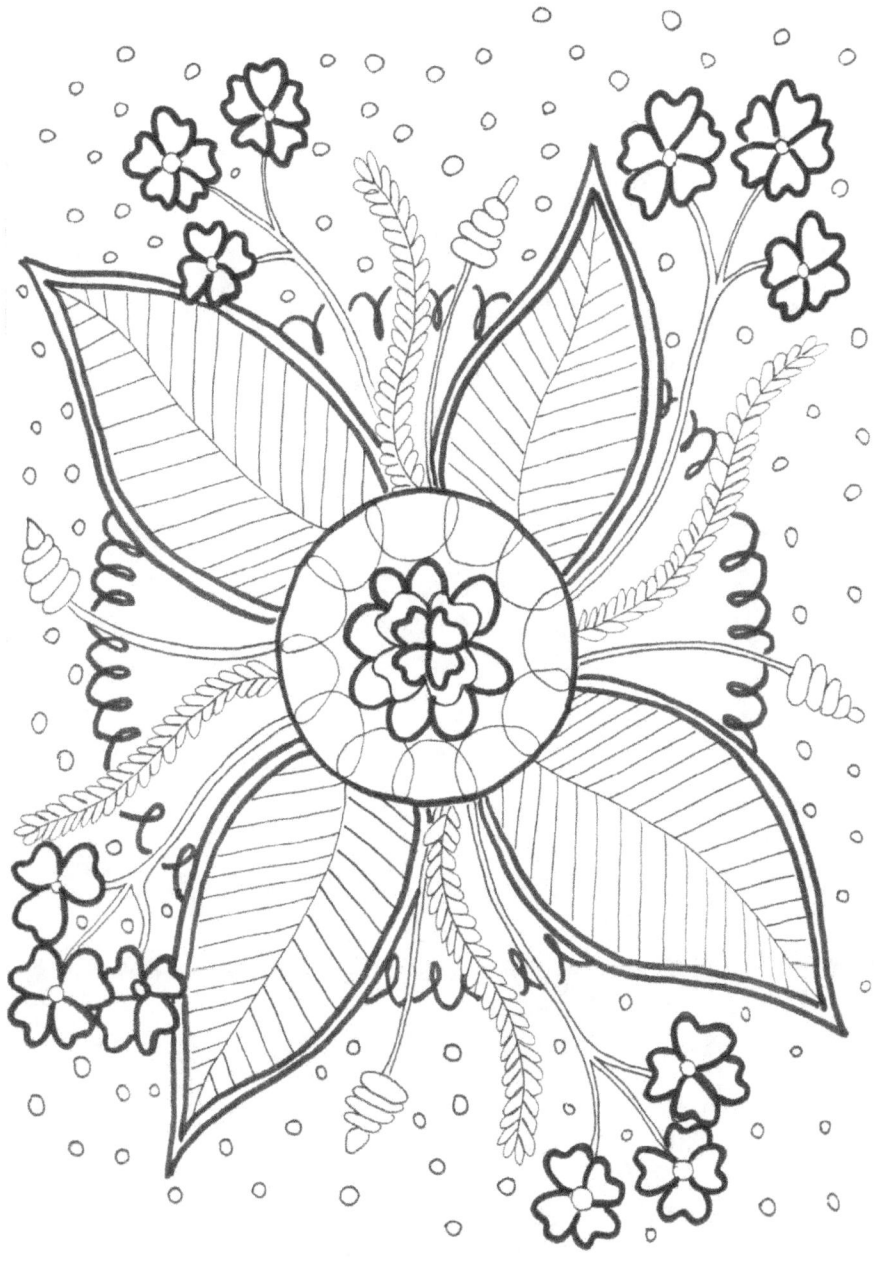

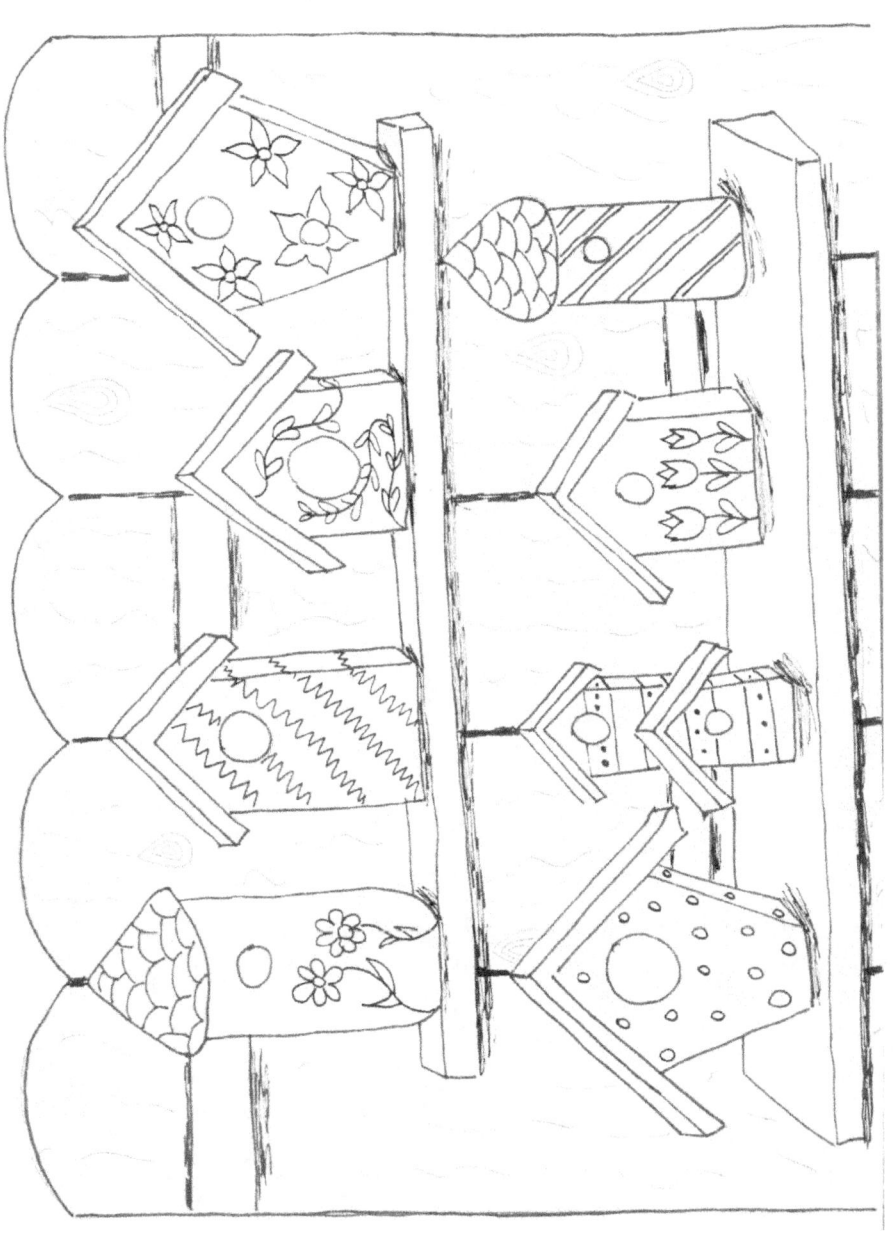

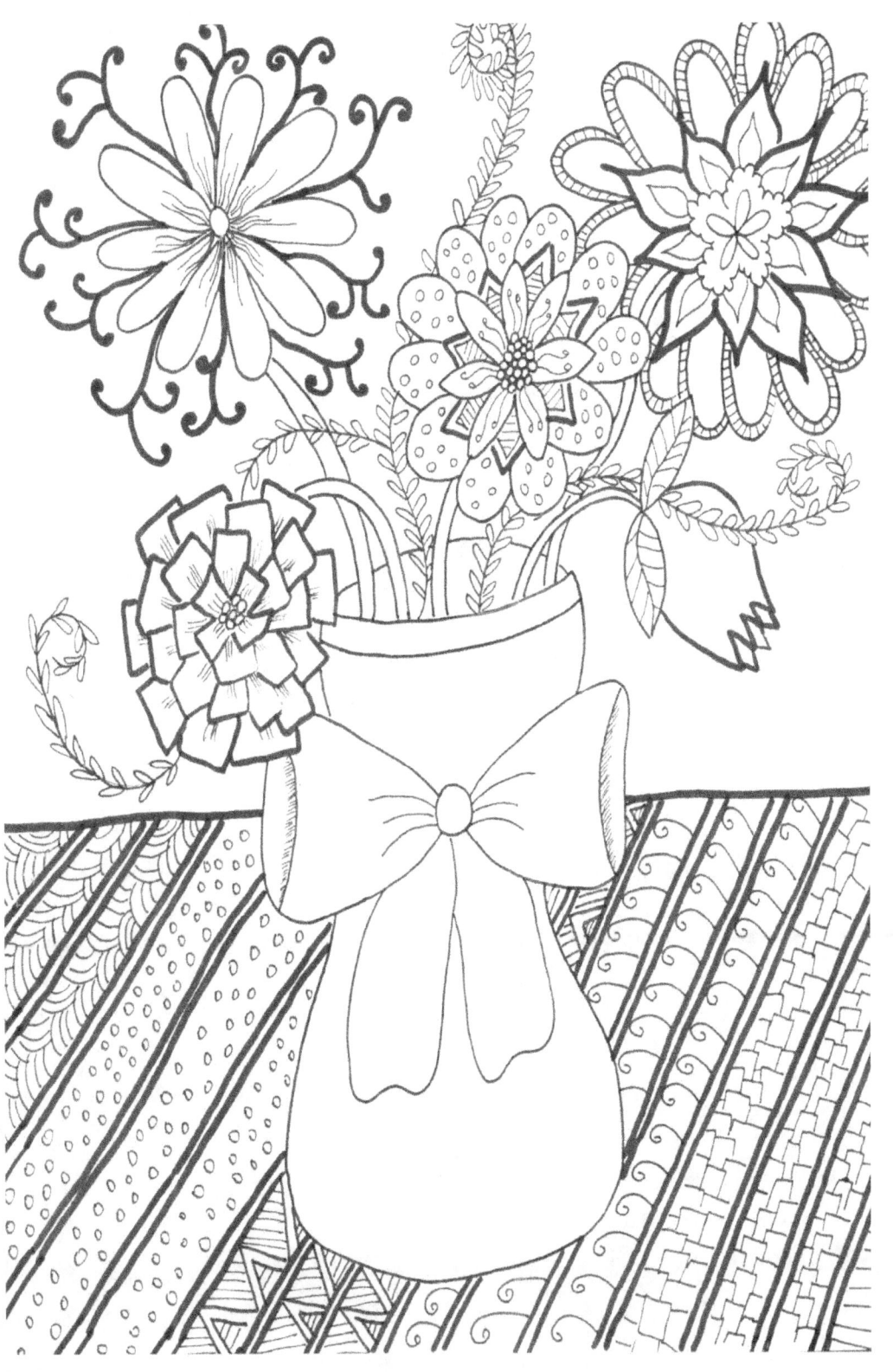

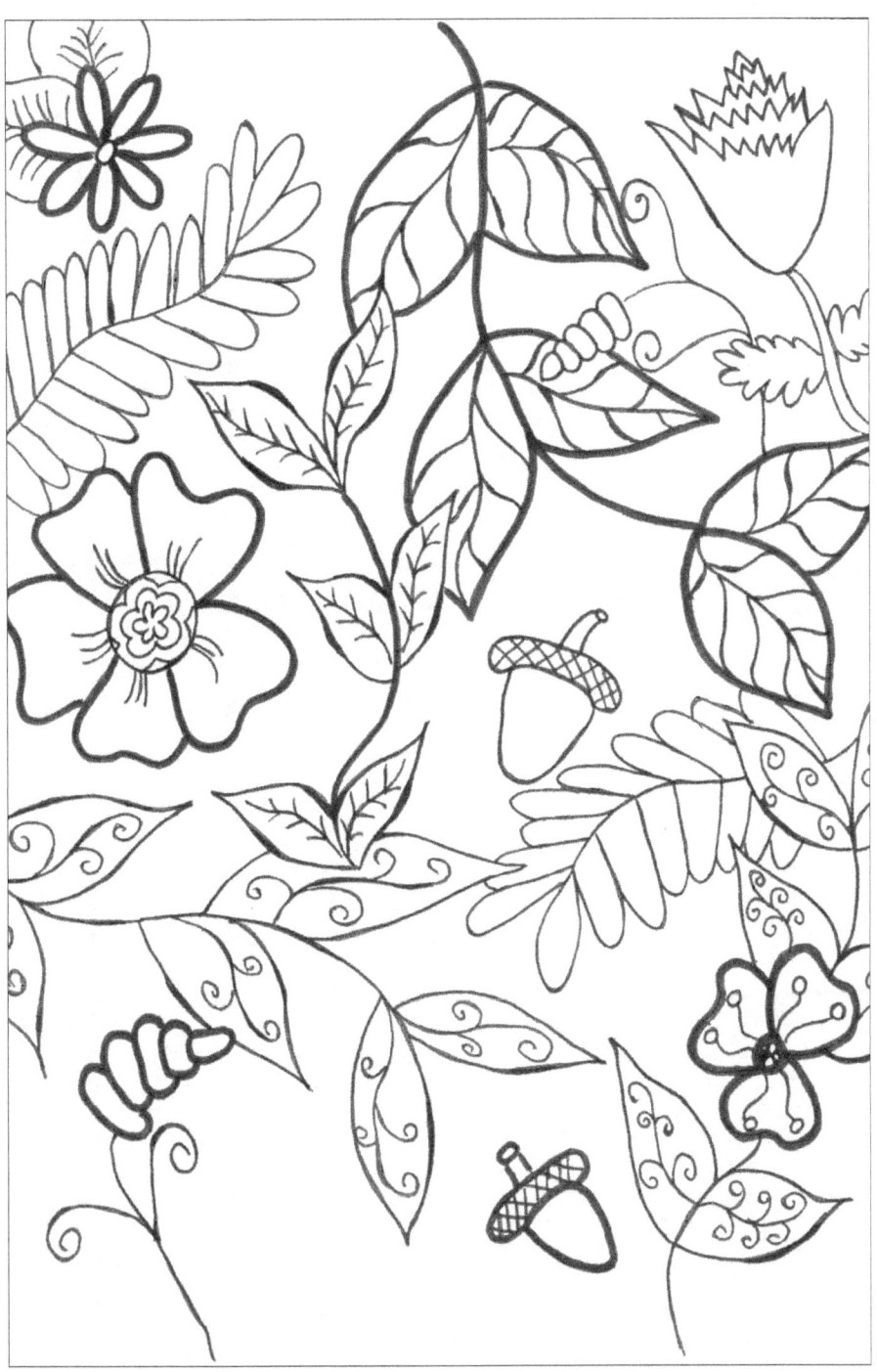

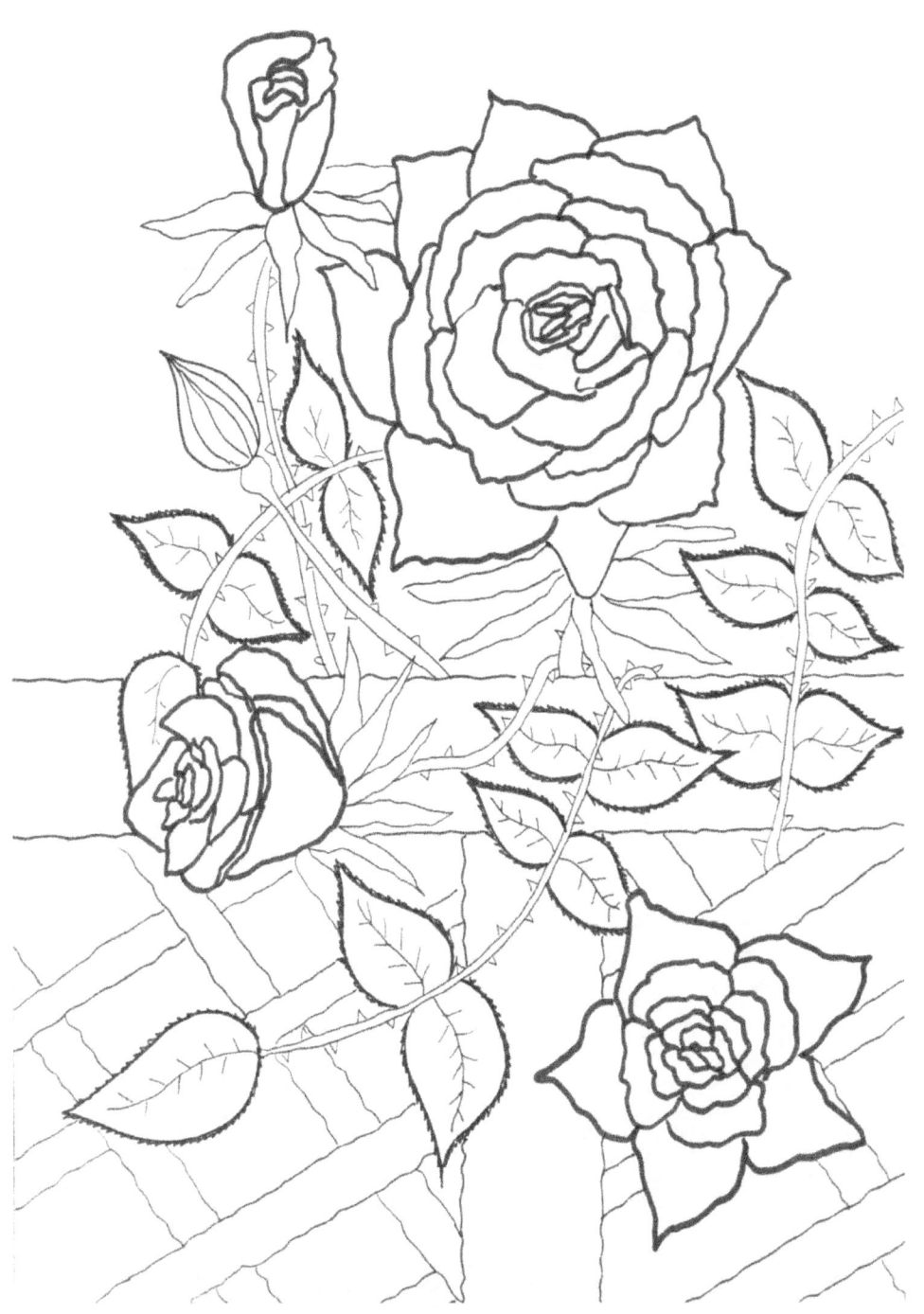

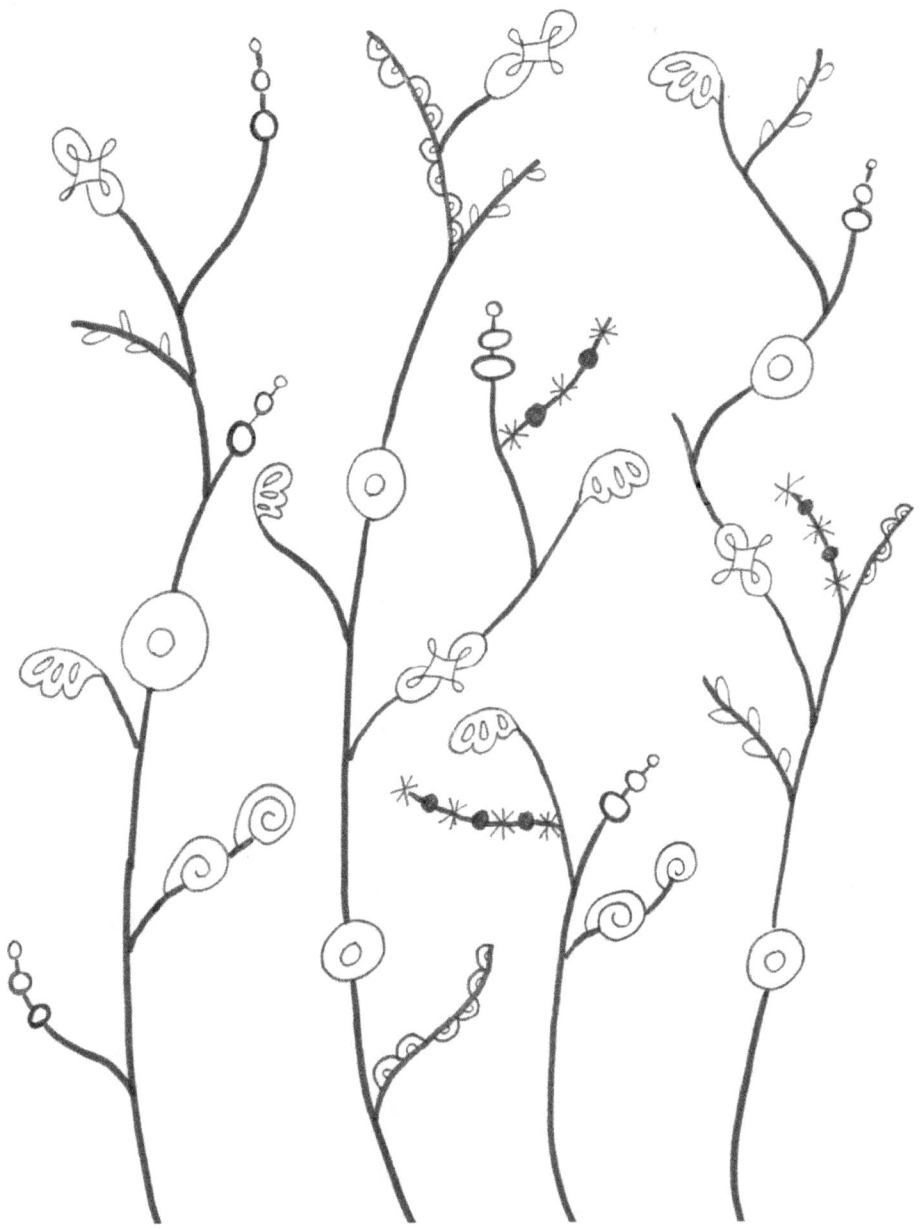

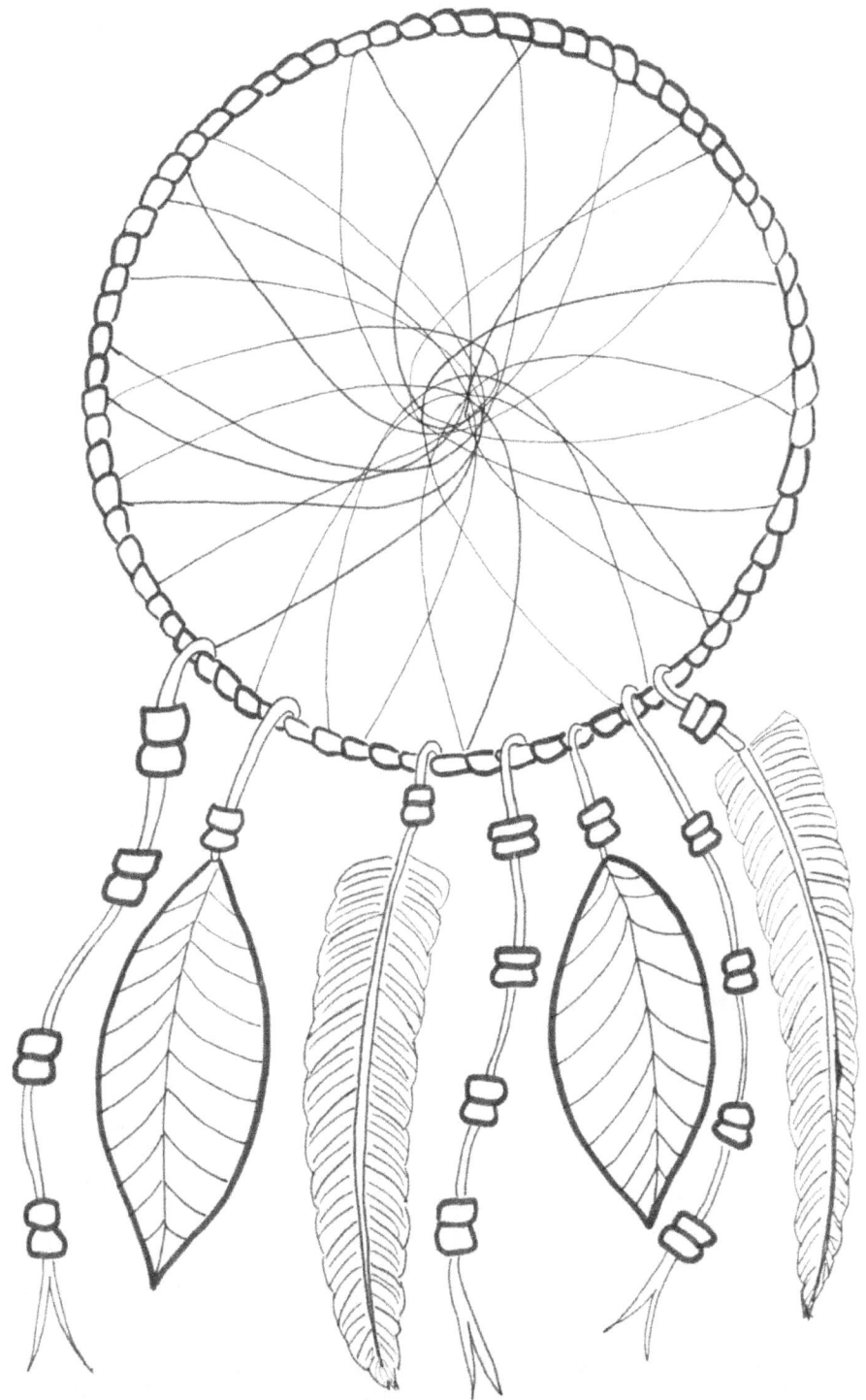

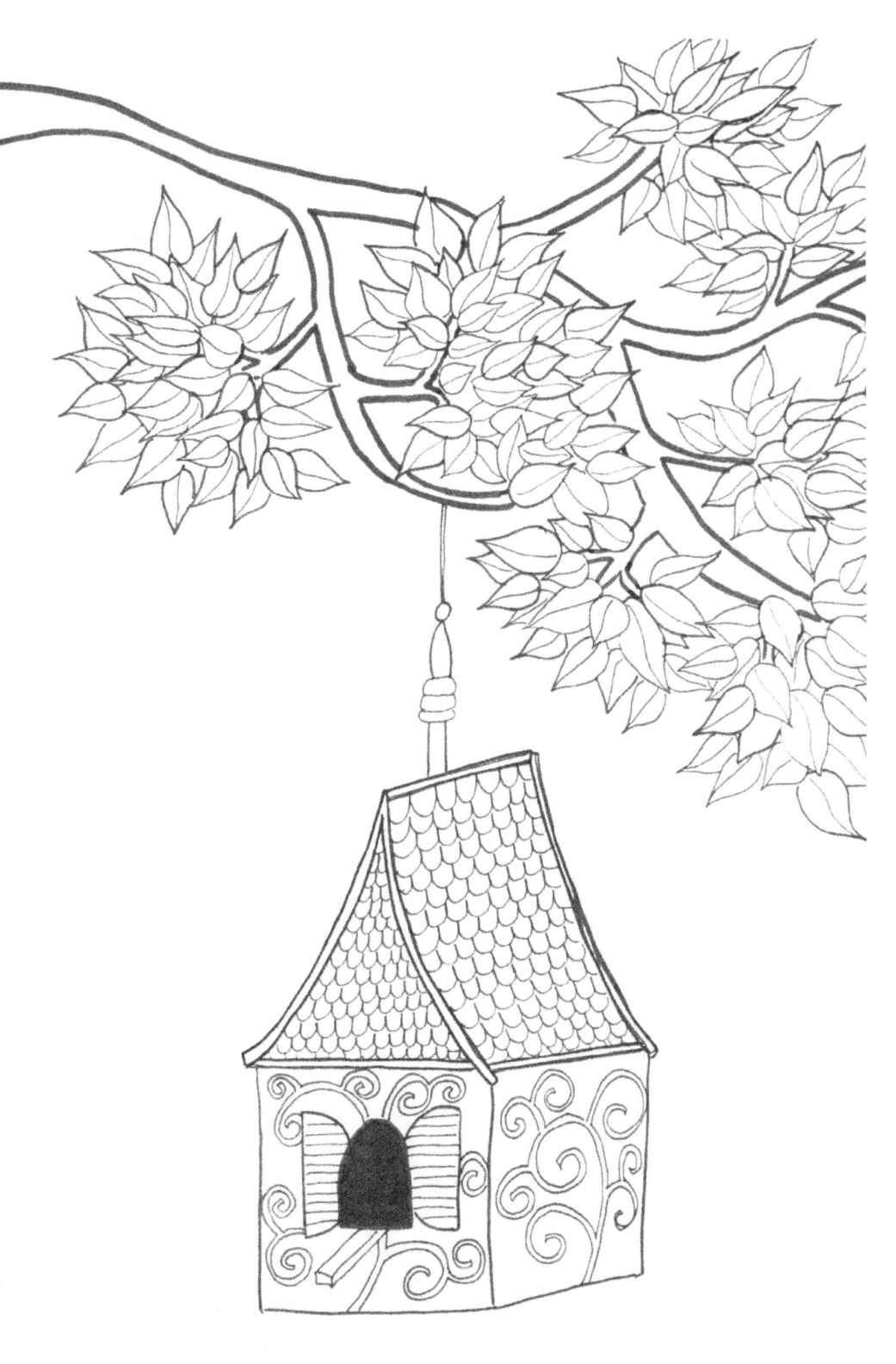

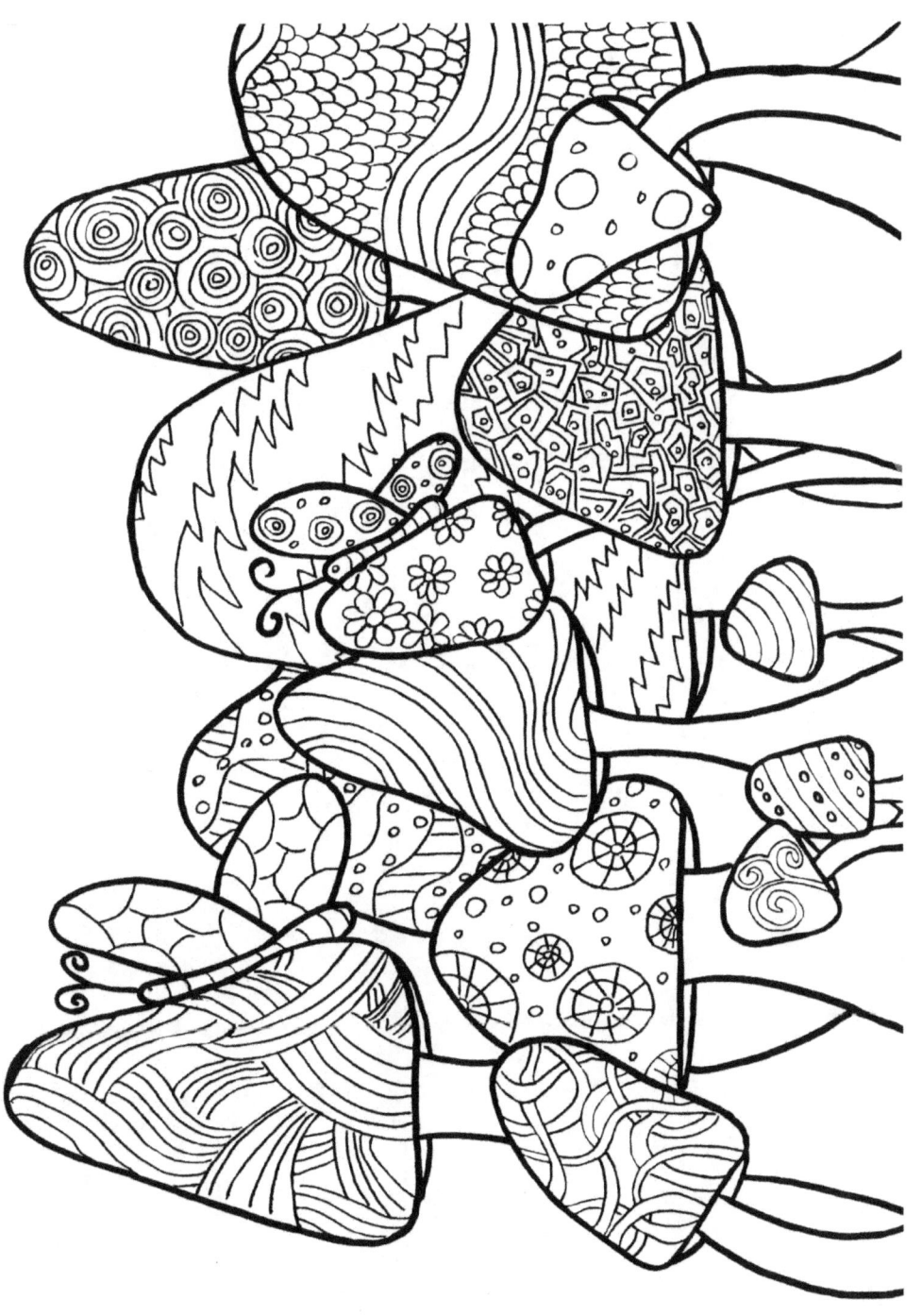

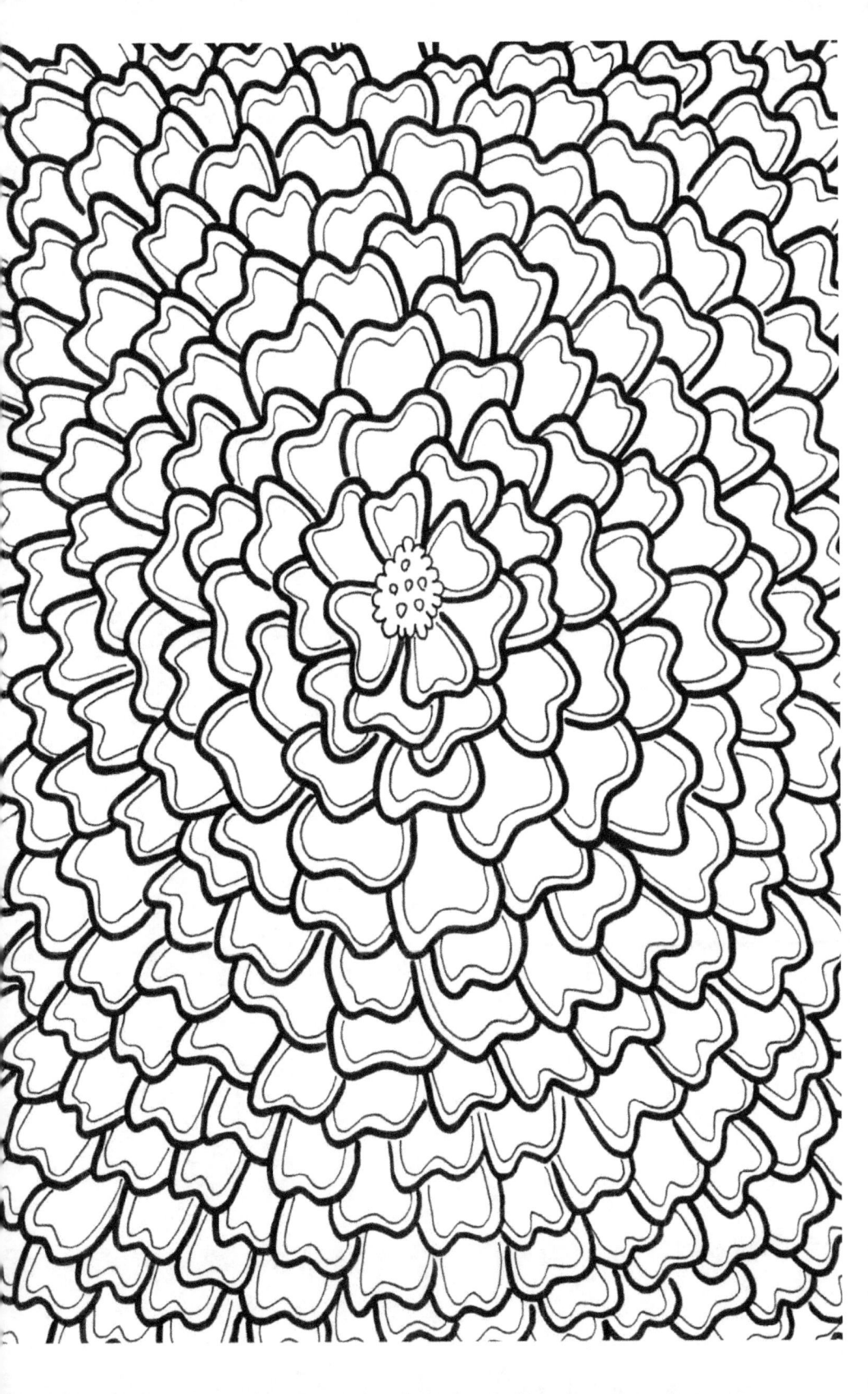

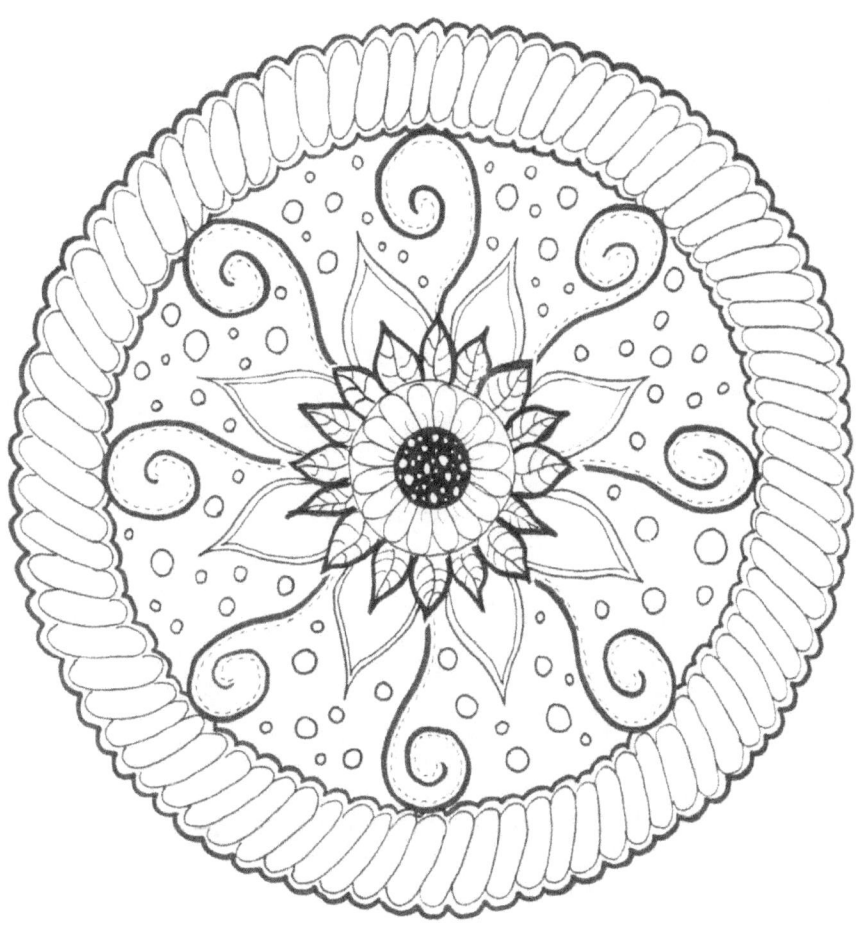

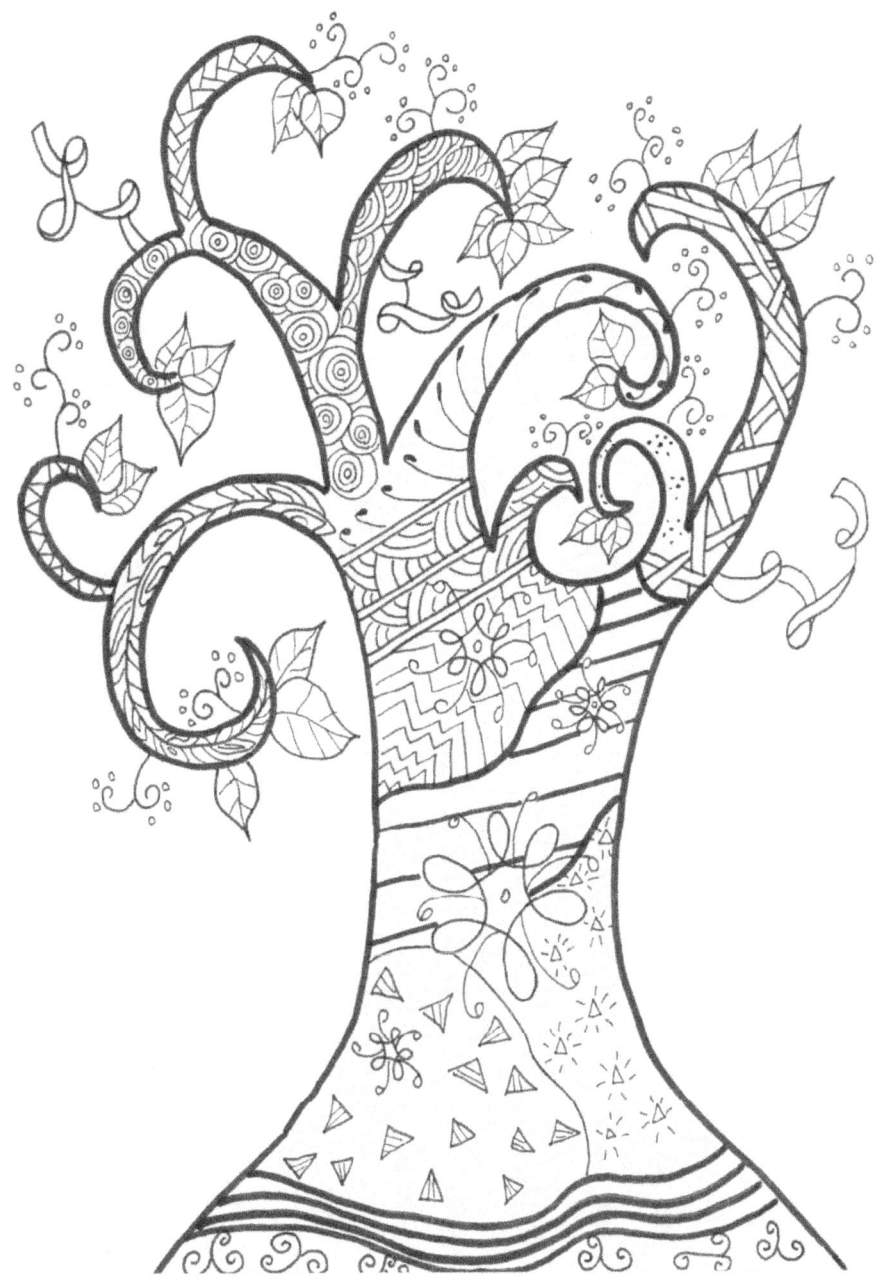

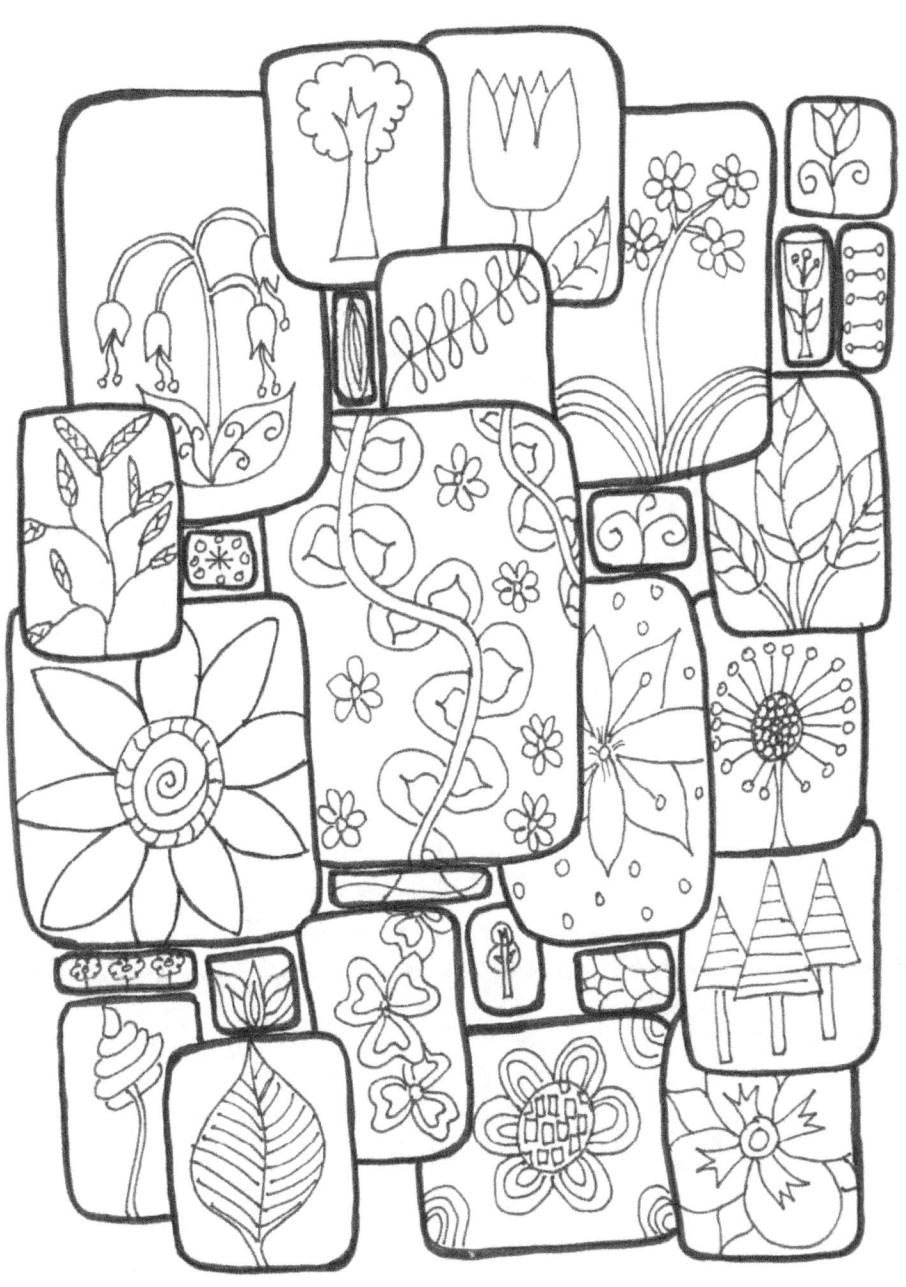

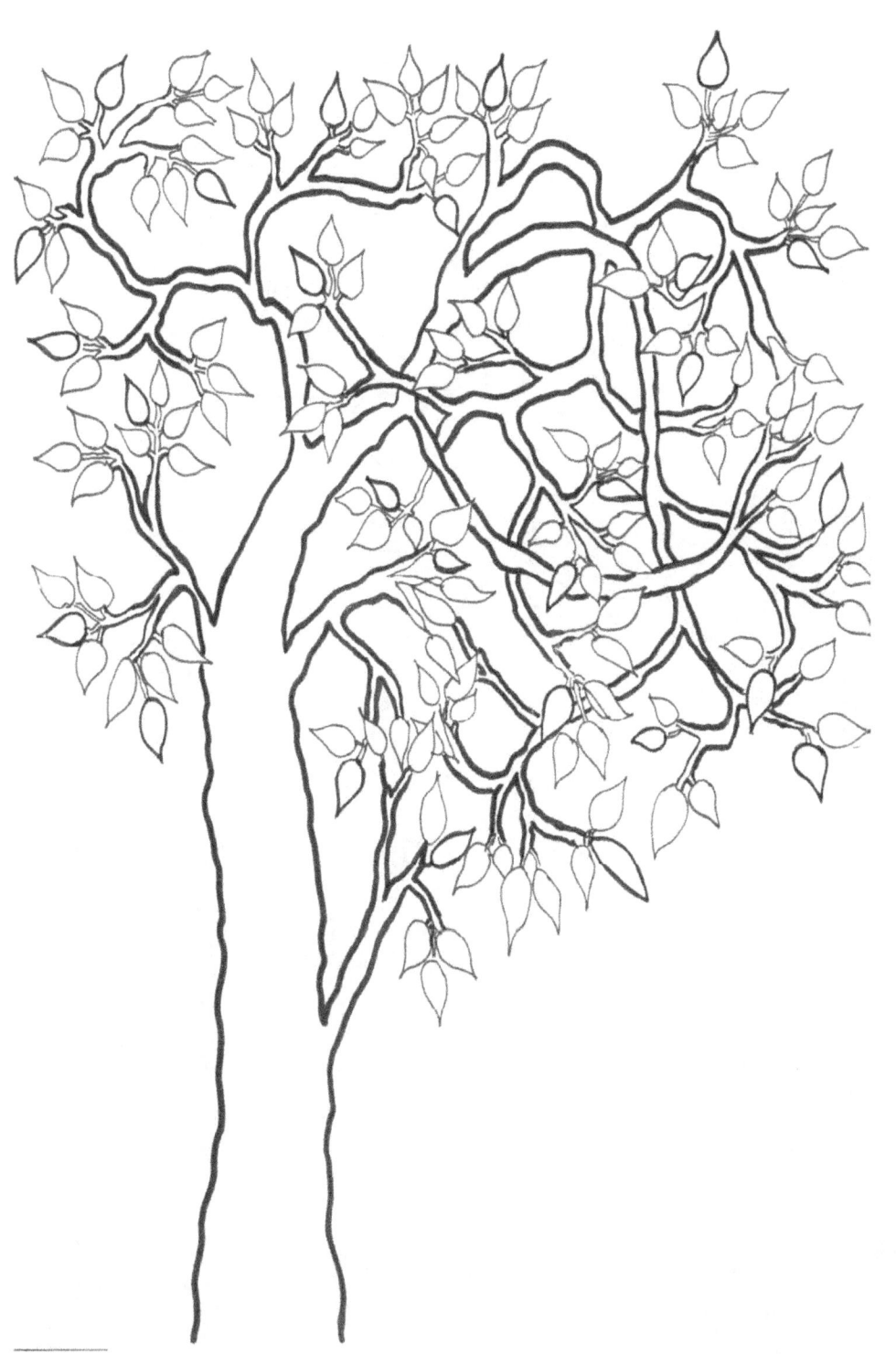

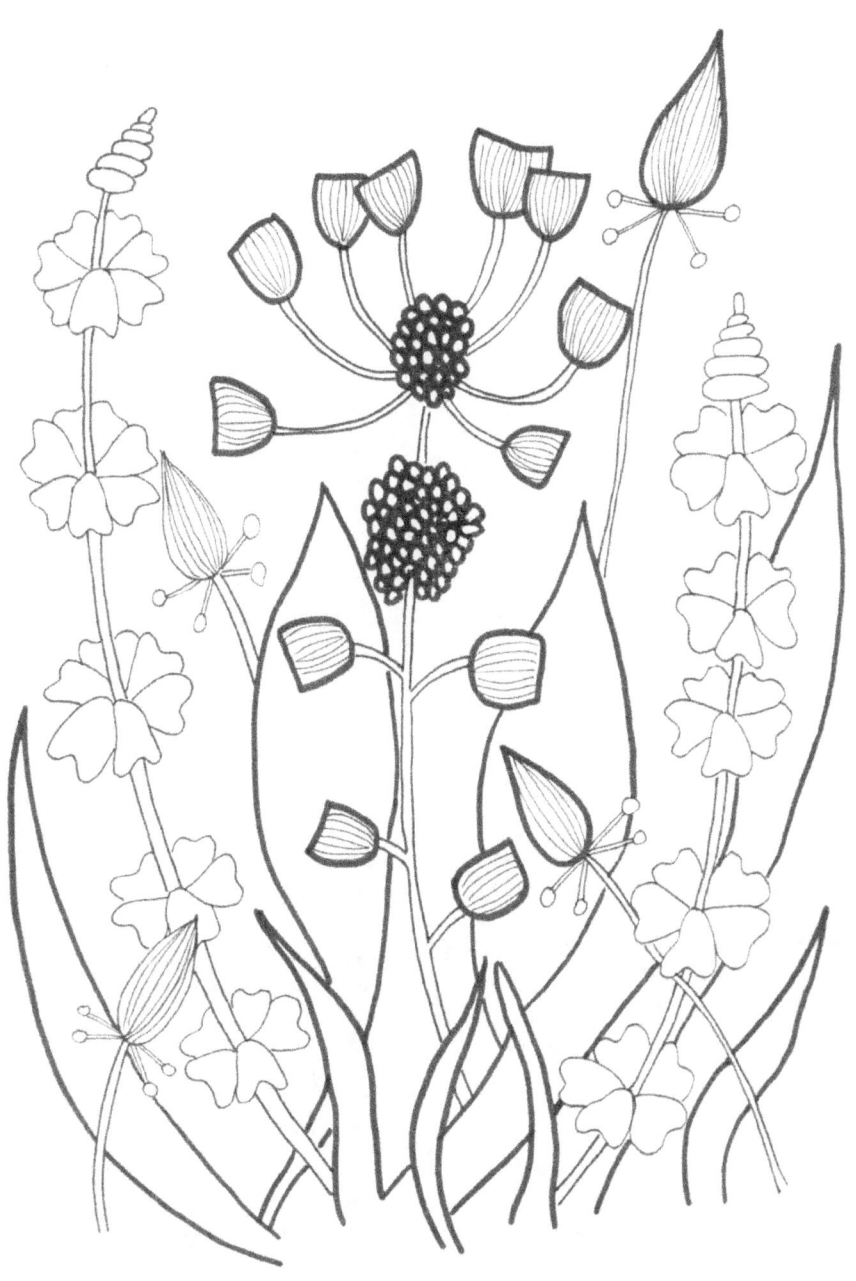

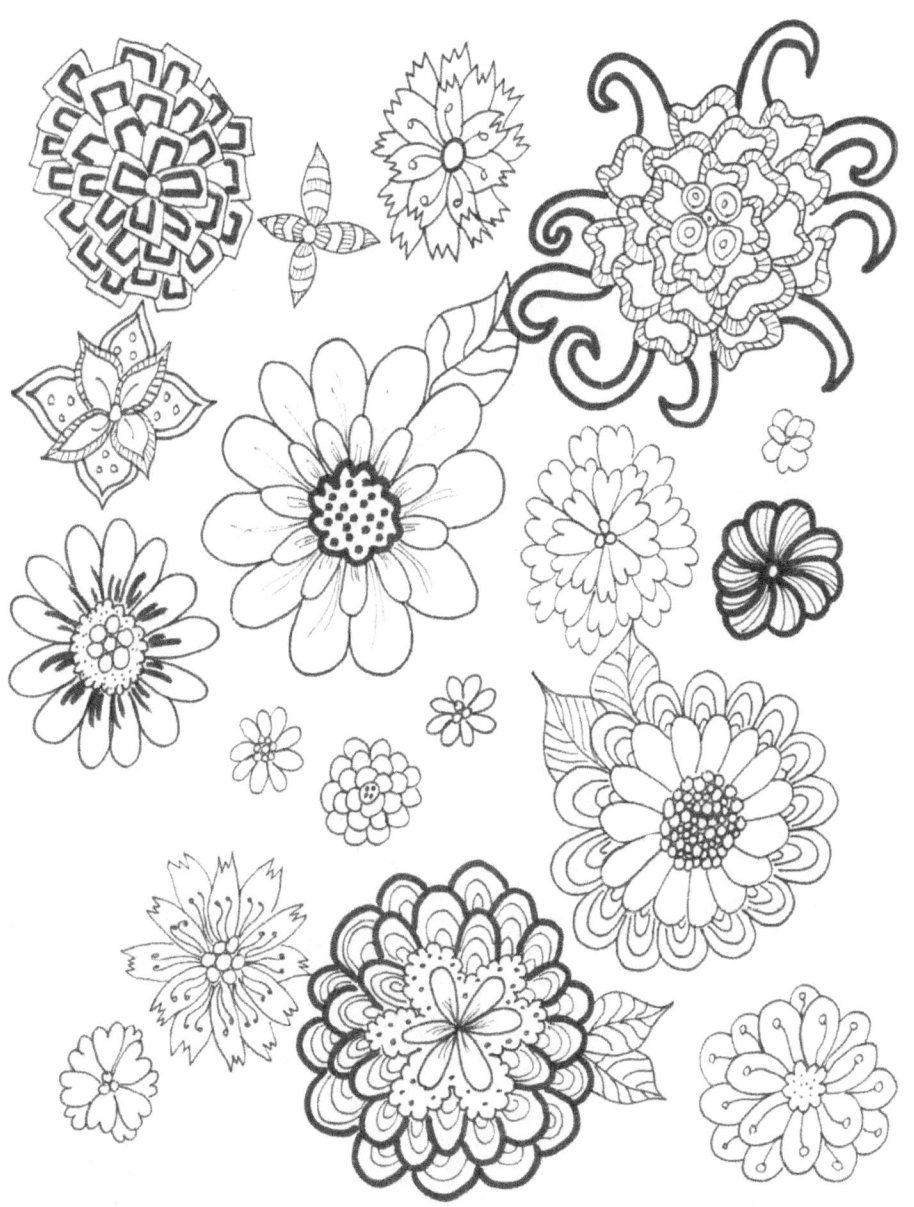

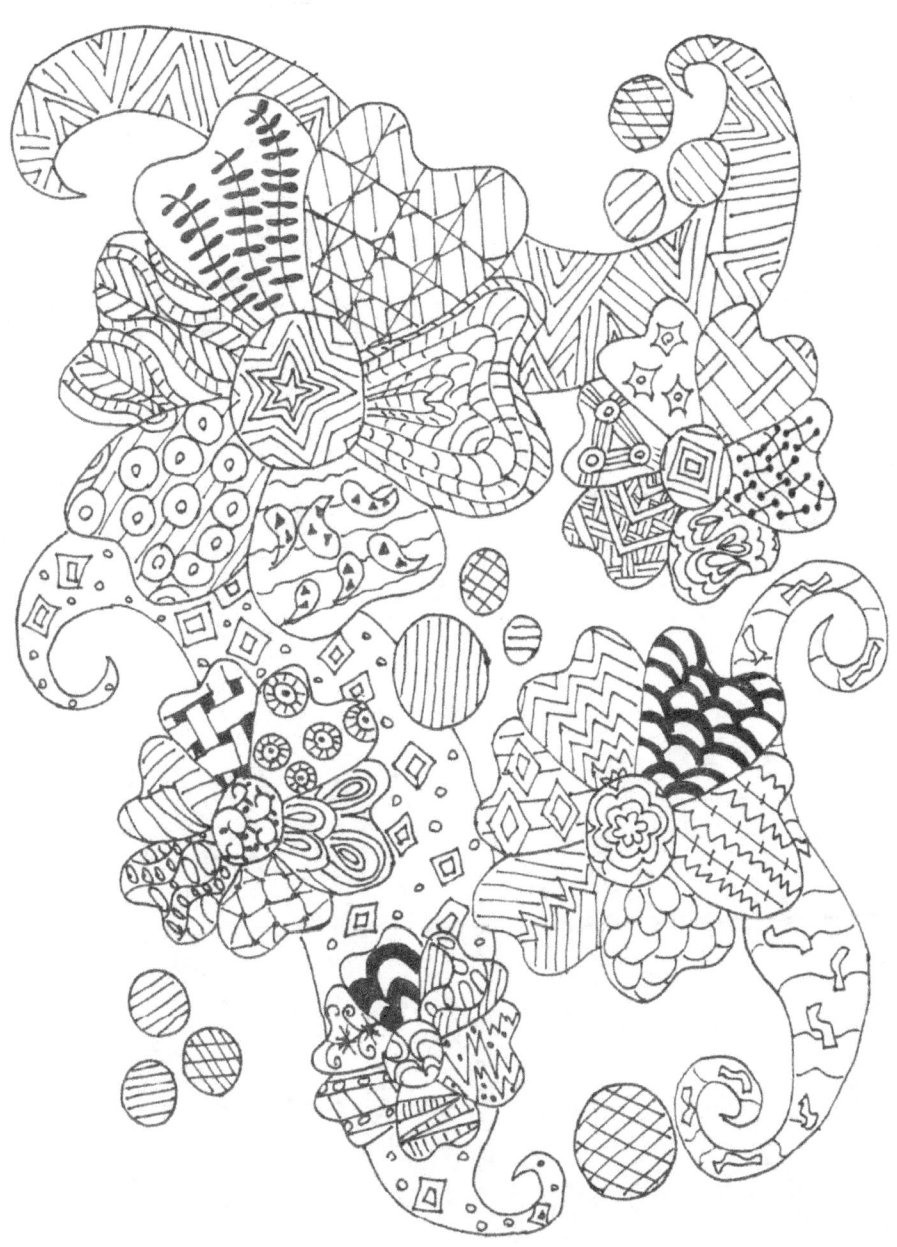

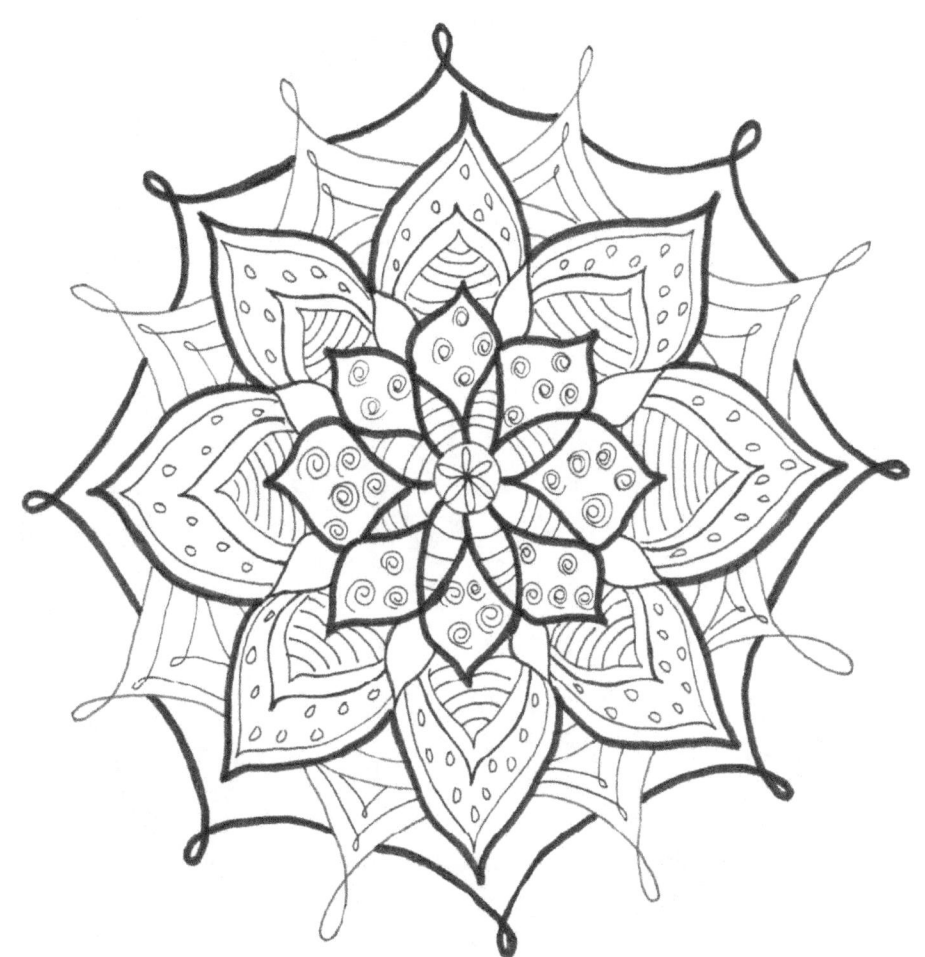